An Astronaut's LIFE

Pebble® Plus

SPACE TRAVEL

by Martha E. H. Rustad

CAPSTONE PRESS
a capstone imprint

Pebble Plus is published by Capstone Press,
1710 Roe Crest Drive, North Mankato, Minnesota 56003
www.mycapstone.com

Library of Congress Cataloging-in-Publication data is available on the Library of Congress website.
ISBN 978-1-5157-9818-7 (library binding)
ISBN 978-1-5157-9822-4 (paperback)
ISBN 978-1-5157-9826-2 (eBook PDF)

Editorial Credits
Abby Colich, editor; Kyle Grenz, designer; Tracy Cummins, media researcher;
Kathy McColley, production specialist

Photo Credits
Getty Images: AFP/KIRILL KUDRYAVTSEV, 5; NASA Image and Video Library: 7, 11, 13, 15, 17,
19; Shutterstock: 3Dsculptor, Cover, 9, Alones, 21, Aphelleon, Design Element, d1sk, Back Cover,
Design Element, Zakharchuk, Design Element

Note to Parents and Teachers

The An Astronaut's Life set supports science standards related to space. This book describes and
illustrates space travel. The images support early readers in understanding the text. The repetition
of words and phrases helps early readers learn new words. This book also introduces early readers
to subject-specific vocabulary words, which are defined in the Glossary section. Early readers may
need assistance to read some words and to use the Table of Contents, Glossary, Read More, Internet
Sites, Critical Thinking Questions, and Index sections of the book.

Printed and bound in the USA.
122018   000057

Table of Contents

Takeoff

Three. Two. One. Blastoff!

You are going to space.

How will you get there?

Let's find out about

space travel.

Takeoff is in a few hours.

The crew boards the spacecraft.

The inside seems small. It is full

of equipment. Workers look over

the spacecraft. They make sure it is safe.

Roar! The takeoff is loud.
The spacecraft shakes. The astronauts
rock in their seats. The spacecraft goes
faster and faster. In about three minutes,
the crew leaves Earth behind.

In space there is less gravity.

Everything floats.

Many people feel sick.

After a few days, they feel better.

But their noses stay stuffy.

Spacecraft

The spacecraft has two parts. One part is the capsule. It's where the astronauts ride. Supplies also fill the capsule.

The other part has very strong rockets. They push the spacecraft away from Earth.

A pilot flies the spacecraft.
Buttons, switches, and screens
fill the dashboard. The pilot steers
up, down, right, and left.
The spacecraft can even roll over.

Today most astronauts go to

a space station. They live and work there.

The space station flies around Earth.

It does not have a dashboard.

People steer it from Earth.

Astronauts stay in space for a few months.

Then it's time to leave. They board the capsule.

It moves toward Earth. Soon gravity

pulls it in. Parachutes slow it down.

The landing is bumpy.

Future Space Trips

Astronauts may soon go to Mars.

They will travel nine months to get there.

The crew will need enough food.

They will need fuel and supplies.

Would you like to travel to space?

GLOSSARY

capsule (KAP-suhl)—a small craft that holds astronauts or other travelers

crew (KROO)—a team of people who work together

dashboard (DASH-bord)—a panel with controls for a vehicle

gravity (GRAV-uh-tee)—a force that pulls objects with mass together; gravity pulls objects down toward the center of Earth

parachute (PAIR-uh-shoot)—a large piece of strong, lightweight fabric that flies out behind a spacecraft during landing; the parachute helps slow down the spacecraft

spacecraft (SPAYSS-kraft)—a vehicle that travels in space

space station (SPAYSS STAY-shuhn)—a spacecraft that circles Earth in which astronauts can live for long periods of time

READ MORE

Gregory, Josh. *If You Were a Kid Docking at the International Space Station.* New York: Children's Press, 2018.

Lakin, Patricia. *The Stellar Story of Space Travel.* History of Fun Stuff. New York: Simon Spotlight, 2016.

Yomtov, Nel. *Sailing the Solar System: The Next 100 Years of Space Exploration.* Our World, the Next 100 Years. North Mankato, Minn.: Capstone, 2017.

INTERNET SITES

Use FactHound to find Internet sites related to this book.

Visit *www.facthound.com*

Just type in 9781515798187 and go.

Check out projects, games and lots more at
www.capstonekids.com

CRITICAL THINKING QUESTIONS

1. Name one part of a spacecraft and describe what it does.

2. Reread the text on page 12 and look at the photo on the opposite page. In which part of the spacecraft are the astronauts located?

3. Reread the text on page 18. What do you think would happen if parachutes did not help the spacecraft slow down?

INDEX